A World of Food

ITALY

Jane Bingham

D0549263

W
FRANKLIN WATTS

First published in paperback in 2015

First published in 2010 by Franklin Watts

Franklin Watts
338 Euston Road
London NW1 3BH

Franklin Watts Australia
Level 17/207 Kent Street, Sydney, NSW 2000

Produced by Arcturus Publishing Limited,
26/27 Bickels Yard, 151–153 Bermondsey Street, London SE1 3HA

Series concept: Alex Woolf
Editor: Alex Woolf
Designer: Jane Hawkins
Map illustrator: Stefan Chabluk
Picture researcher: Alex Woolf

Picture Credits
Art Archive: 6 (Bardo Museum, Tunis/Gianni Dagli Orti).
Bridgeman Art Library: 7 (Osterreichische Nationalbibliothek, Vienna/Alinari).
Corbis: 4 (Jonathan Blair), 9 bruschetta (Desgrieux/PhotoCuisine), 11 (Jeffrey L Rotman), 12 (Sandro Vannini), 13 (Massimo Borchi/Atlantide Phototravel), 14 (Hussenot/PhotoCuisine), 15 (Stephanie Maze), cover and 16 (Jonathan Blair), 17 (Owen Franken), 20 (Vittoriano Rastelli), 22 (Hubert Stadler), 23 bottom (Owen Franken), 24 (Stuart Freedman), 26 right (Sandro Vannini), 27 (Ivan Vdovin/JAI), 28 (Bernd Thissen/dpa), 29 (Richard Cummins).
Getty Images: 8 (Hulton Archive/Keystone/Stringer).
Shutterstock: 9 ciabatta (ulga), 9 mozzarella, basil and garlic (Stefano Tiraboschi), 9 olive oil and balsamic vinegar (cen), 10 (Claudio Giovanni Colombo), 18 (Massimiliano Pieraccini), 19 (Cristy), 21 cinnamon (Ariy), 21 wooden spoon with flour (adam36), 21 eggs (Matthew Cole), 21 almonds (Elnur), 21 biscotti (ultimathule), 23 top (Igor Dutina), 25 onion (Marcio Maitan Alberico), 25 garlic clove (Chernyanskiy Vladimir Alexandrovich), 25 rosemary (Drozdowski), 25 bay leaves (Elenamiv), 25 tomato tin (Pennyimages), 25 spaghetti con pomodoro (Elenamiv), 26 left (David P Smith), 31 ravioli (Iwona Grodzka).

A CIP catalogue record for this book is available from the British Library.

Dewey Decimal Classification Number: 394.1'2'0945

ISBN 978 1 4451 4489 4

Printed in China

Franklin Watts is a division of Hachette Children's Books, an Hachette UK company.
www.hachette.co.uk

SL001038UK
Supplier 29, Date 0315, Print run 4037

Contents

Buon Appetito!

Italy is famous for its delicious food. People all over the world enjoy Italian pizzas and pasta – two national dishes that come in dozens of different forms. In fact, pizzas and pasta are just a tiny part of the amazing variety of foods that make up Italian cuisine.

Famous foods

Apart from its world-famous pizzas and pasta, Italy is known for its range of preserved meats, such as Parma ham and salami. Italian bread is also very popular, especially ciabbata, a flat, crispy loaf often used for sandwiches.

Italian farmers grow olives and produce fine wines. They also make some great cheeses, including

▲ Food is a very important part of Italian life. This family are sharing a meal after a hard day's work.

mozzarella (a soft cheese used for pizza toppings), Parmesan (a hard cheese, often used for grating over pasta dishes) and Gorgonzola (a strong-tasting cheese with blue veins running through it).

Tomatoes, onions and garlic are used in many Italian sauces, and Italian cooks like to flavour their food with herbs, especially basil, oregano and rosemary.

Pasta galore!

Italy has over a hundred varieties of pasta, but they can be divided into five main types. The list below gives two examples of each type of pasta:
- pasta tubes – macaroni and rigatoni (ridged tubes)
- pasta ribbons – tagliatelle and fettuccine
- pasta strings – spaghetti and vermicelli (very thin pasta strings used in soups)
- pasta shapes – farfalle (butterflies) and *conchiglie* (shells)
- pasta parcels – ravioli and tortellini

SOME COMMON ITALIAN FOODS

Word	Pronunciation	Meaning
carne	CAR-neh	meat
pesce	PESH-ay	fish
uova	oo-WOH-vah	eggs
formaggio	FOR-maj-ee-oh	cheese
frutta	FROO-tah	fruit
verdure	VER-door-eh	vegetables
insalata	IN-sal-ah-tah	salad
latte	LAT-eh	milk

▼ This map of Italy shows the locations of some of the places mentioned in this book.

History of Italian Food

People in Italy have enjoyed wonderful food for thousands of years. As early as the 4th century BCE an Italian poet was giving good advice to cooks. He said that they should always use fresh ingredients and warned against adding too many spices or herbs.

◄ This mosaic shows a Roman banquet. A serving boy carries a dish on his head and musicians entertain the guests.

ROMAN SURPRISES

Guests at a Roman banquet were sometimes served some very surprising dishes. One Roman chef created a bird's nest from pastry and filled it with eggs made from sausage meat. Another chef made a pig's belly look just like a fish!

Roman food

From 30 BCE to 476 CE, Italy was at the heart of the Roman Empire. Most poor people ate very basic food, such as bread and porridge. Richer Romans ate lots of fruit, bread, cheese and eggs, and a little meat and fish.

Really wealthy Romans held grand banquets with many courses. Banquets often included very unusual dishes, such as dormice in honey, elephants' trunks and flamingoes' tongues.

Medieval flavours

During the medieval period, from around 500 to 1400 CE, several invaders arrived in Italy, bringing new ingredients and ways of preparing food. Tribes from Germany settled in northern Italy and introduced the practice of curing meat to preserve it. (See page 23 for more about curing.)

▼ Italians have eaten spaghetti for more than 800 years. This picture shows spaghetti-making in the 14th century.

Arabs conquered Sicily in the 9th century, bringing Eastern ingredients such as rice, spinach and almonds. Between 1130 and 1204, Sicily and southern Italy were ruled by Normans, who came from northern France. The Normans introduced casseroles and stews to southern Italy.

Pasta probably had its origins in southern Italy in the Middle Ages. In the 12th century, some Normans recorded that people in Sicily were eating long strings made of flour and water – a food that was later known as spaghetti.

Colourful Ingredients

From the 1490s, Italian explorers reached North and South America. They brought back new foods, such as tomatoes, peppers, potatoes and maize.

Italian cooks created some exciting dishes using these ingredients. In particular, tomatoes became an important part of Italian cooking. They were used for pasta sauces and pizza toppings.

Pizza for a queen

In 1889, an Italian chef created a special pizza for Queen Margherita of Savoy. For the topping he chose ingredients that were coloured red, white and green, like the stripes on the Italian flag. Queen Margherita's pizza was covered with *red* tomatoes, *white* mozzarella cheese, and *green* basil leaves. Later it became known as a pizza Margherita.

▶ In the 1950s, pizzas were sold in the street by pizza boys.

RECIPE: bruschette tricolore

This recipe has the same topping as a pizza Margherita, but its base is made from slices of bread.

Equipment
- breadboard and knife • chopping board and knife • small mixing bowl

Ingredients (for 6 slices)
- 3 large, ripe tomatoes • extra virgin olive oil
- balsamic vinegar • salt and pepper
- 1/2 small packet of mozzarella cheese
- small loaf of ciabatta bread (or a small cottage loaf) • 3 garlic cloves, peeled and cut in half • 1 handful of roughly chopped basil leaves

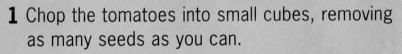

1 Chop the tomatoes into small cubes, removing as many seeds as you can.

2 In a bowl, mix the tomato cubes with 1 tablespoon of olive oil and a few drops of vinegar.

3 Season the tomato mixture with salt and pepper.

4 Chop the mozzarella cheese into small pieces.

5 Cut the bread into thick slices and grill until both sides are lightly browned.

6 Rub a garlic half over the top side of each of the bread slices.

7 Drizzle olive oil over the slices.

8 Spread the tomato mixture over the slices and scatter with small pieces of mozzarella.

9 Grill the slices until the mozzarella starts to melt.

10 Remove from the grill and decorate with chopped basil leaves.

Land of Plenty

Italy forms a long peninsula of land stretching into the Mediterranean Sea. Many people think it looks like a boot.

The Italian countryside is mainly hilly, but it also has two high mountain ranges known as the Alps and the Appenines. The Alps run from west to east along the country's northern border. The Appenines run from north to south down the spine of Italy.

Sunshine and snow

The climate of Italy is extremely varied. In the coastal regions and the south, the weather is mild all year round. The southernmost tip of Italy and the islands of Sardinia and Sicily have very hot, dry summers. Winters in the north can be extremely cold, with thick snow on the mountains.

▼ The rolling hills of Tuscany are ideal for growing wheat and grapes.

Farming and fishing

Italy's farmers grow a wide range of produce. In the dry, sunny south, they concentrate on olives, fruit and vegetables. The gentle hills are used for wheat fields and vineyards, and the lower mountain slopes provide good pasture for cattle. Farmers in the north grow cereals and rice in the valley of the River Po.

FRIDAY FISH

Many people in Italy choose to eat fish rather than meat on Fridays. In the past, leaders of the Roman Catholic Church insisted that all Catholics should eat fish on Fridays. This religious tradition still continues in some country areas, and is especially strong in places by the sea.

Italy has over 6,400 kilometres of coastline, as well as many rivers and lakes. With all this water, it is not surprising that fishing is very important. Fish caught off the shores of Italy include tuna, swordfish, anchovies and sardines. Italian fishermen also catch octopuses and squid, lobsters and shrimps, and collect a wide range of shellfish, such as clams, scallops, mussels and oysters.

▶ These Sicilian fishermen are hauling in a massive catch of tuna.

Food from Farms

The main crops grown in Italy are wheat and maize. Wheat is used for making bread and pasta. Most Italian farmers grow durum wheat, a type of hard wheat that is especially good for making dried pasta and dry, crispy breads such as ciabatta.

Maize and rice

Maize is ground up and boiled to make a kind of porridge called polenta. In northern Italy, polenta is often eaten in place of potatoes, or made into dumplings. It is also used instead of flour in cakes.

Some farmers grow a special variety of rice, known as Arborio. It has short, fat grains containing a lot of starch. When it is cooked, Arborio rice becomes rich and creamy and is perfect for risottos.

Meat and dairy farming

Italian farmers rear cows and pigs for their meat. A few rear lambs, but lamb is not a very common meat in Italy. Dairy cattle are very important for producing Italy's famous cheeses, and farmers also make cheese from sheep's and goats' milk. In southern Italy, farmers keep herds of water buffalo, which produce high-quality mozzarella cheese.

◀ Mozzarella cheese is made in large kettles. It has to be stirred constantly.

Fruit and vegetables

Italian farmers grow a wonderful range of fruit and vegetables. There are vineyards all over the country producing grapes for red and white wine. Apple orchards are found in the north and citrus trees in the south, and some southern farmers specialize in peaches, apricots and melons.

Vegetables grown in northern Italy include pumpkins, asparagus and radicchio (a leafy vegetable with red leaves). Southern Italians grow tomatoes, courgettes, aubergines, spinach and peppers, as well as a range of pulses, such as lentils and beans.

▲ Italian markets have excellent fruit and vegetable stalls. This one is in Bologna.

WILD MEALS

In the mountainous regions of the north, people eat a lot of game (wild animals and birds that are hunted and shot). Dishes made from rabbits and hares are especially popular.

Eating the Italian Way

Italians take cooking and eating seriously. An Italian family meal will usually have at least three courses, and formal meals have many more.

The five courses described below make up a traditional Italian meal. People sometimes choose to skip the antipasto or one of the last two courses, but they always keep the *primo* and *secondo*.

Antipasto, primo and secondo

Italian meals often begin with an antipasto. The name means 'before the meal' and the antipasto is meant as an appetizer to prepare people for the main meal. Olives, cold meats and marinated vegetables are often served as an antipasto. Soup is also a popular antipasto, and can vary from a clear broth, often containing noodles, to a hearty dish made with beans, vegetables and meat.

▼ Ravioli, tortellini and spaghetti are popular choices for the *primo*.

The *primo*, or first course, is generally the most filling dish of the meal. It is often some kind of pasta or risotto, a dish made mainly from rice. Next comes the *secondo*, or second course, which is usually meat or fish. A salad or cooked vegetables are served separately as a side dish. This side dish is called a *contorno*.

Formaggio e frutta and dolce

After the *secondo*, people eat a selection of cheeses and fruit (*formaggio e frutta*). Then they move on to the *dolce* or 'sweet'. This may be cakes or biscuits, or an Italian dessert such as tiramisu – a rich sweet made from cream and sponge cake soaked in coffee.

▶ This Italian family is enjoying a lengthy lunch with several courses.

COFFEE TIME

Many Italians like to finish their meal with a small cup of strong black coffee, called a *caffè* or an espresso. Italians also enjoy other types of coffee, such as *caffè latte* (white coffee) or cappuccino (white coffee topped with frothy milk), but they do not drink coffee with milk after 11 am.

Of course, people in Italy do not always have the time for a five-course meal. When they want something quick and easy to eat, families often share a pizza. Italians can also choose from a range of excellent 'fast foods'.

Different pizzas

There are two main kinds of pizza on sale in Italy. Takeaway shops sell slices of *pizza al taglio*. This kind of pizza is cooked on a large metal tray and then cut into rectangles. Pizzerias (pizza restaurants) sell

▼ A pizza chef in Amalfi prepares a new batch of pizzas to be cooked in the oven.

circular pizzas, with a very thin, crispy base. Circular pizzas are usually cooked in a stone oven over an oak-wood fire.

Sometimes, the circular pizza bases are folded over to form a kind of envelope. These pizza-envelopes are known as calzoni. They often contain vegetables and meat mixed with a soft cheese such as ricotta (see page 27).

(see page 27)

PIZZA VARIETIES

Here are just a few of the many different pizzas you can buy in Italy, with a list of the ingredients used for their toppings:

- pizza *capricciosa* – tomatoes, mozzarella, mushrooms, artichokes, ham, olives, olive oil
- pizza Margherita – tomatoes, mozzarella, basil, olive oil
- pizza *marinara* – tomatoes, garlic, oregano, olive oil
- pizza *romana* – tomatoes, mozzarella, anchovies, oregano, olive oil

All sorts of snacks

Italians have some delicious snacks to choose from. They can buy a panini – a sandwich made from a small loaf of bread that tastes especially good when it is heated up. Or they can choose a slice of focaccia – a flat, soft bread that is usually seasoned with olive oil and herbs.

Crostini are made from small slices of bread toasted under a grill and rubbed with garlic and olive oil. They are served with a variety of toppings, such as tomatoes, cheese, olives and ham.

▶ Many Italians buy their panini from a baker and make their snacks at home.

Most people in Italy are members of the Roman Catholic Church, and religious festivals are a very important part of Italian life. Christmas and Easter are the main festivals of the year. People prepare and eat special foods for these important occasions.

Christmas treats

It is traditional for Catholics to fast (eat no food) for 24 hours before Christmas. Then, on Christmas Eve, they eat a light dinner. For this dinner, people avoid meat, and eat fish and seafood. Cod and eel are popular favourites for Christmas Eve, and some families eat dishes made from snails and frogs.

On Christmas Day, Italians often start their meal with tortellini (see page 24). This is followed by a meat dish, such as roast chicken or turkey stuffed

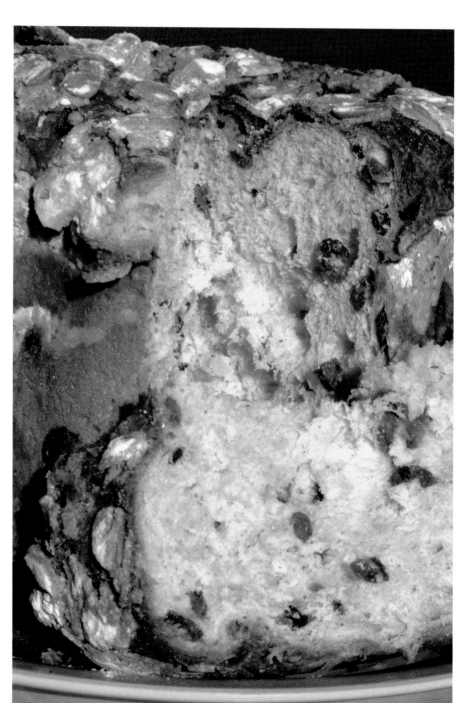

▶ Panettone is very light and fluffy. Once you've started eating it, it is hard to stop!

with chestnuts. Italians also eat panettone, a traditional Christmas dessert. Panettone is a tall, circular loaf of sweet-tasting bread, which contains raisins and pieces of candied peel. Another popular Christmas dessert is *pandoro*, a sweet bread dusted with icing sugar.

Food for Easter

For their Easter Sunday meal, most Italians eat roast lamb and traditional Easter breads. The meal ends with special cakes. A common Italian Easter cake is the *colomba*, made in the shape of a dove, the symbol of peace. In Tuscany and Umbria, people have a special Easter breakfast with salami, boiled eggs and pizzas.

► In Bormio in the Italian Alps, young people dress in traditional costumes each Easter and carry painted eggs in a procession through the town.

TONI'S BREAD?

Panettone comes from the city of Milan and dates back at least 500 years. According to one legend, it was invented by a kitchen boy called Toni who worked for the Duke of Milan. The story relates that Toni created the cake from leftover bread dough, after the special Christmas dessert had been burned. The duke loved the new dessert and insisted that it be called *pane di Toni*, or 'Toni's bread'.

Saints' Days

In Italy, people celebrate special saints' days. Some of these celebrations are national festivals, such as All Saints' Day on 1 November. Others are feasts for local saints.

On All Saints' Day, people eat dishes made from peas or lentils. They end their meal with sweet biscuits known as *ossi di morto*, or 'bones of the dead'.

Food for Saint Joseph

On the island of Sicily, people celebrate Saint Joseph's Day. There is an ancient legend that Saint Joseph once saved the islanders from starvation, and every 19 March they give thanks to him. The Sicilians hold a feast for everyone on the island. They cook special breads, biscuits and *zeppole* (deep-fried cakes rather like doughnuts).

▶ Sicilians have several traditional festival days. Here, a group of musicians entertain the crowds on Saint Rosalia's Day.

RECIPE: biscotti

Biscotti are sweet biscuits that are cooked for festivals.

Equipment
- large mixing bowl • wooden spoon • medium-sized mixing bowl • fork • wooden board, dusted with flour • rolling pin • knife • 2 metal baking trays, greased with butter and dusted with flour

Ingredients (for about 25 biscotti)
- 180g castor sugar • 260g plain flour
- 2 large eggs • 1 level teaspoon baking powder
- 1 teaspoon cinnamon
- 100g whole unblanched almonds • 1 teaspoon vanilla essence

1. Preheat the oven to 180°C.

2. In the large mixing bowl, mix flour, sugar, baking powder, cinnamon and almonds.

3. In the other bowl, use a fork to whisk together the eggs and vanilla essence.

4. Stir this mixture into the large bowl, then use your hands to make a ball of stiff dough.

5. Turn the dough onto the floured wooden board.

6. Use a rolling pin to roll out a thick shape 12 cm wide x 24 cm long.

7. Cut the shape in half lengthways to make two strips.

8. Place strips on the baking trays and bake for 25 minutes, until firm.

9. Remove from the oven and allow to cool.

10. Slice diagonally into biscuits about 2cm wide.

11. Place biscuits flat on the baking sheet and bake for another 15 to 20 minutes, until golden brown.

People living in northern Italy eat a lot more meat than Italians in the south. The northern regions are famous for their many varieties of pasta, their cured (preserved) meats and their cheeses.

▲ Polenta is mainly eaten in northern Italy. It looks like a thick, yellow porridge.

Food in the Alps

The northernmost regions of Italy are part of the Alps mountain range. In winter, people need to keep warm so they usually eat hearty, filling food, such as sausages and stews. Pork is the most popular meat, and butchers sell cured sausages, bacon and ham. Typical foods of the alpine regions are goulash (a kind of spicy stew), cheese fondue (a dish in which chunks of bread are dipped in hot, liquid cheese) and roasted chestnuts.

The people of the Italian Alps often use beans in their cooking. They make dumplings from polenta, and gnocchi (small dumplings) from potatoes. Dishes in these regions show the influence of the country's neighbours to the north: Switzerland, Austria and Croatia.

Cured meats

Most of Italy's cured meats come from the north. The northern regions produce salami (a strong-tasting sausage made from chopped-up meat) and prosciutto (very thin slices of cured, raw ham). The most famous variety of prosciutto is made in the town of Parma, and known as Parma ham.

Sausages and hams are cured by hanging them in a cold, dry environment for up to 18 months. During this time, the meat dries out and its flavour becomes much stronger.

MOULDY CHEESE

Gorgonzola cheese is a speciality of Piedmont and Lombardy. The cheese is allowed to age for three to four months, with metal rods inserted into it. The rods make air channels where mould can germinate, creating blue-coloured veins in the cheese. The result is a very strong tasting, slightly crumbly cheese.

▲ A slice of Gorgonzola cheese.

▶ Some northern specialities: Parmesan cheese, cured meats, a plate of Parma ham and a bottle of red wine.

Pasta and Parmigiano

Some of Italy's most famous pasta dishes come from the region of Emilia-Romagna in northern Italy. Dishes from this region include tortellini and lasagne.

Tortellini are ring-shaped pasta parcels, traditionally stuffed with minced meat. Lasagne is made with alternate layers of pasta, cheese sauce and bolognese sauce (see below).

Bolognese sauce

The city of Bologna is the home of bolognese sauce. Traditional bolognese sauce is made from minced beef, onions, carrots, celery, tomato paste and red wine, and includes some cured bacon known as pancetta.

▲ These chefs are making tortellini for Bologna's most famous pasta shop, Le Sfogline.

In the city of Bologna, bolognese sauce is usually served with tagliatelle (a ribbon pasta). It is sprinkled with grated *parmigiano* (Parmesan), a hard cheese made in the Emilia-Romagna region.

RECIPE: spaghetti con pomodoro

Spaghetti with tomato sauce is popular all over Italy. It should be served with plenty of Parmesan cheese.

Equipment
- chopping board and knife • garlic crusher
- frying pan and spatula • large saucepan with steep sides • colander for draining spaghetti
- cheese grater

Ingredients (serves 4)
- 4 tablespoons olive oil
- 1 small onion, finely chopped
- 2 x 400g tins of chopped tomatoes
- 1 clove garlic, crushed
- leaves from a sprig of rosemary, finely chopped
- 2 fresh bay leaves • salt and pepper
- 500g dried spaghetti • Parmesan cheese, grated

1 Heat the oil in the frying pan, add the chopped onion and cook over a very low heat for 5 minutes until soft but not brown.

2 Stir in the tomatoes, crushed garlic and rosemary.

3 Add the bay leaves and cook over a low heat for 30 minutes until the sauce is very thick.

4 Season with salt and pepper.

5 Add the spaghetti to the pan of boiling water and cook for around 10 minutes until it is still a little chewy.

6 Drain the spaghetti and stir it into the sauce.

7 Serve topped with lots of grated Parmesan cheese.

Dishes from the South

People in southern Italy eat a lot of fish and seafood. They grow a great variety of vegetables and fruit and use large quantities of garlic and olive oil in their cooking.

Southern specialities

In the regions of Abruzzo and Molise, on the east coast of Italy, cooks often flavour their food with chillies. Calabria, in the 'toe' of Italy, is famous for its seafood and its melons. Sometimes melon slices are served wrapped in prosciutto (very thin slices of cured ham). In Puglia, in the 'heel' of Italy, people often use chickpeas, lentils and beans in their cooking. They also create dishes using the oysters and mussels found on the coast.

The area around Naples is known for its pizzas and its desserts. Neopolitan desserts include *sfogliatelle*, cone-shaped pastries filled with orange-flavoured ricotta

▲ A plate of *sfogliatelle* filled with ricotta.

▶ A baker in Naples rolls out dough for *sfogliatelle*.

(see panel). Another is *pastiera napoletana*, a sweet cake made with ricotta and usually eaten at Easter.

Sicily and Sardinia

Sicily was conquered by Arabs in the 10th century, and its food still shows a strong Arab influence. Sicilian cooks often flavour their food with saffron, nutmeg, cloves and cinnamon. Tuna, sea bream, swordfish and cuttlefish are all used in Sicilian dishes.

The island of Sardinia is famous for its sardines, as well as its scampi, squid and lobster. Pig and wild boar are roasted on spits or boiled in stews with beans and vegetables. Sardinians bake a flat, dry bread, which is often served with tomatoes, fresh herbs and cheese.

RICOTTA

Ricotta is a soft white cheese with a slightly sweet taste. It is made from the liquid (known as whey) that is left behind when milk is turned into cheese. Ricotta is a very popular ingredient in Italian cakes and pastries. It is also often used as part of the filling for calzoni (see page 17).

▼ Sicilian restaurants serve an amazing range of freshly caught seafood.

All Change?

Today, most people in Italy have much less time for cooking than they had in the past. There is a danger that traditional Italian cuisine could disappear – especially in the cities.

Fortunately, however, traditional cuisine remains popular in many places. Regional dishes are still served in restaurants all over Italy, and sharing meals together remains a very important part of Italian family life.

Is it really Italian?

Versions of Italian food can be found far from Italy. In cities all over the world, you can order takeaway pizzas with an amazing range of different toppings. You can also buy Italian-style ready meals and sauces.

▶ Pizza is popular all over the world. Here, German factory workers prepare pizzas to be frozen and sold in supermarkets.

PIZZA FROM HAWAII?

One of the most popular pizzas outside Italy is the Hawaiian pizza – a pizza with a tomato and mozzarella topping, scattered with ham and pineapple chunks. Some people say the Hawaiian pizza was invented on the island of Hawaii. Others claim it was first made in Germany. But wherever it came from, it is certainly not Italian!

The quality of this kind of food varies enormously. Some of it is nothing like the food that people enjoy in Italy!

Discovering Italian food

Many people outside Italy take an interest in Italian food. There are a growing number of good Italian restaurants, where chefs make traditional dishes, using high-quality, fresh ingredients.

Some popular chefs have made TV programmes on real Italian food. For example, Jamie Oliver made a series when he travelled all over Italy learning about regional dishes. There are also many excellent Italian cookery books available in the shops.

Of course, the best way to experience Italian food is to visit Italy and try it for yourself, but it is also possible to cook some really delicious Italian dishes at home.

◀ An Italian restaurant in California. Italians run great restaurants all over the world.

Glossary

anchovies Very small, salty-tasting fish, often preserved in oil.

antipasto The first part of a meal that acts as an appetizer (see below).

appetizer A small dish that prepares the eater's appetite for the main meal.

artichoke A vegetable with many leaves, often eaten by dipping each leaf into olive oil.

broth Clear soup.

calzoni Folded-over pizzas that contain their ingredients in a kind of envelope.

casserole A stew cooked slowly at a low heat in a covered pot or dish.

Catholics Members of the Roman Catholic Church (see below).

ciabbata A flat, crispy bread that is often used to make sandwiches.

cuisine A way of preparing and cooking food.

curing A way of treating food to stop it from going bad, by drying it and smoking it.

dumplings Balls made from a substance such as polenta or potato, that are included in a casserole or stew.

ingredient One of the food items that a dish is made from.

marinated Soaked in oil, vinegar or another substance.

mozzarella A soft, white cheese, often used for pizza toppings.

Parmesan A hard cheese, often used for grating over pasta dishes.

peninsula A piece of land sticking out into the ocean, surrounded on three sides by water.

polenta A kind of porridge made from maize.

preserve Treat food in a special way so that it will last for a long time.

prosciutto Raw ham that has been cured for around 18 months and cut into very thin slices.

pulses Beans, peas or lentils.

ricotta A soft, white cheese made from the liquid that is left behind when milk is turned into cheese.

risotto A dish made mainly from rice, mixed with other ingredients such as vegetables and fish.

Roman Catholic Church A branch of the Christian Church that is led by the pope in Rome.

seafood Fish or shellfish that can be eaten as food.

starch A substance found in foods such as rice, bread and pasta.

vineyards Fields where grapes are grown.

Further Information

Books

Festive Foods: Italy by Sylvia Goulding (Chelsea Clubhouse, 2008)

Italy: World of Recipes by Julie McCulloch (Heinemann Library, 2002)

National Geographic Countries of the World: Italy by Robert Anderson (National Geographic Children's Books, 2006)

A Taste of Culture: Foods of Italy by Barbara Sheen (Kidhaven Press, 2005)

Websites

www.foodbycountry.com/Germany-to-Japan/Italy.html
Food in Italy: General information about Italy, and recipes.

www.food-links.com/countries/italy/italian-food-culture.php
Italian Food and Culture: Information about the history of Italian cuisine, and the typical dishes of each region.

www.kidport.com/Reflib/WorldGeography/Italy/Italy.htm
Italian Geography: Illustrated information about Italy organized by topics such as history, geography culture

kids.nationalgeographic.com/Places/Find/Italy
National Geographic Kids: Facts, photos and videos about Italy.

Index